Auto Scaling Cooldown

Configuration and Challenges

Table of Contents

Chapter 1. Introduction

The following Special Report delves into the vital and nuanced world of Auto Scaling Cooldown, a feature that is essential in maintaining a balanced and well-functioning cloud infrastructure. Oriented towards both beginners and seasoned tech professionals, this report meticulously unpacks the ins and outs of configuring Auto Scaling Cooldown and outlines the potential challenges that may be encountered during this process. Written in accessible, down-to-earth language, the report strives to present the technicalities in a digestible manner, allowing even the non-tech-savvy readers to understand and appreciate the mechanisms behind this important aspect of auto scaling. Buckle up and get ready to explore the nitty gritties of a solution that is making waves in the cloud computing world.

Chapter 2. Introduction to Auto Scaling and Cooldown

Before we dive into the heart of auto scaling and its cool down mechanics, it is crucial to frame our discussion within the context of cloud computing. The era of cloud computing has truly begun, radically transforming the IT landscape. The benefits are immense: high availability, cost-effectiveness, dynamic resource management, and unmatched scalability, to name a few. The walls of physical constraints are collapsing, replaced with the amorphous and boundless potential of the cloud.

One particular feature standing at the forefront of this revolution is auto-scaling, a simple yet powerful tool that is becoming increasingly central to the efficient functioning of a cloud-based system.

2.1. What is Auto Scaling?

In layman terms, auto scaling is an approach to dynamically allocate or de-allocate the resources as per the real-time demand. It is a means to optimize resource usage and maintain the performance of your applications, even during a sudden surge or dip in traffic.

The goal is not to keep a bunch of machines running all the time, but to have just enough to meet the current demand. The beauty of auto scaling is that it accommodates both crescendos and decrescendos of resource demand, helping businesses walk the tightrope of cost-effectiveness and peak performance.

Auto scaling hinges on two main types of scaling: horizontal scaling and vertical scaling. Horizontal scaling, also known as "scale-out", involves adding or removing instances to handle the load, while vertical scaling or "scale-up" increases resources in an existing instance.

2.2. The Need for Auto Scaling

Auto scaling comes into the picture when you seek to automate resource management. Suppose you have a web application running on a single server. If a sudden traffic surge occurs, your lonely server faces an overload, leading to deteriorating performances or even a full-on crash. Conversely, if the traffic is way less than what your server can handle, it simply lounges around, wasting resources.

Consider the ubiquitous retail moguls. Their traffic is not consistent; rather, it spikes enormously during holiday seasons, Black Friday, or Cyber Monday. Furthermore, there could be sudden demand surges due to flash sales or the debut of a highly anticipated product. Auto scaling enables such businesses to handle these spikes efficiently without breaking the bank.

2.3. Auto Scaling Components

A typical auto scaling suite consists of three major components:

1. **Groups**: A group is the heart of any auto scaling operation. This is where you define the number of instances that can be created and destroyed.

2. **Configuration Templates**: These are the guiding documents that provide the specifications for instances. Every time the system scales out, it uses these templates to create a new instance.

3. **Policies**: Policies are the triggers for the scaling actions. They define the scale-out and scale-in conditions based on a set of parameters or thresholds.

With the components understood, let's shift our focus to a hidden star of the auto-scaling roster - the cooling down period.

2.4. Towards Understanding Cooldown

A cooldown is essentially a pause, a rest period between two scaling actions to allow the system to stabilize. Why is it necessary? Imagine the bloated workload on Black Friday, prompting your auto scaling policies to add more instances. It takes some time for these instances to launch and start contributing to the workload (also known as latency).

If there were no cooldown period, your system might mistakenly observe that the extra instances haven't eased the load and respond by launching more instances. The result? An uncontrolled spiral of instance creation, leading to resource wastage and possible performance degradation.

Setting up a cooldown period gives your system the time to leverage the newly added resources before making further scaling decisions. It variates between applications, use cases, and mostly depends on how long a new instance takes to get up and its operational speed.

In the following chapters, we will dive deeper into configuring auto scaling cooldown, the potential issues you might run into, and how to surmount them. By the end, not only will you understand but also appreciate the critical role it plays in maintaining the stability and efficiency of cloud services, underpinning the dynamic and cost-effective nature of contemporary IT infrastructure.

This is just the tip of the iceberg. The world of auto scaling – with its checks and balances, its marvelous capabilities, and complexities – is vast and intriguing. And the reward for comprehending this multifaceted feature is a resilient, high-performance, cost-optimized system – the ultimate goal of any business in the cloud computing era.

And so, as we journey deeper into the realms of auto-scaling and cool down, hold onto your curiosity. It will be the compass that navigates through the labyrinth of this crucial technology.

Chapter 3. Understanding the Cooldown Period and Why It Matters

Auto Scaling is an essential element in the world of cloud computing. It allows companies to scale resources up or down based on the load or any defined conditions, providing flexibility, business continuity, and cost-efficiency. One of the primary components within the auto scaling framework is the Cooldown period. This plays a crucial role in maintaining a balance within the cloud infrastructure, preventing excessive and unnecessary scaling activities.

3.1. What Is a Cooldown Period?

At its core, the Cooldown period is a predetermined length of time that an auto scaling group waits before it initiates another scaling activity. This is especially important following a scaling action such as launching or terminating instances. This period allows the system to stabilize and the effects of previous scaling activities to fully manifest before another action is taken.

The Cooldown period is measured in seconds, and it begins immediately following the completion of a scaling activity. The default value for most cloud service providers, like Amazon Web Services (AWS), is 300 seconds, although this can be adjusted according to the needs of the system.

3.2. Significance of the Cooldown Period

The Cooldown period carries significant importance in auto scaling for several reasons. Key among them are:

- `Capacity Management`: The Cooldown period plays a vital role in preventing over-scaling or under-scaling. It provides the necessary time for the system workloads to stabilize before any additional scaling action is initiated, thereby ensuring an optimal number of instances are running at any given time.

- `Cost Efficiency`: Without a Cooldown period, there could be a situation where new instances are continuously launched and terminated, leading to cost inefficiencies. By ensuring a waiting period between scaling activities, the Cooldown period plays a role in cost optimization.

- `Performance Assurance`: The Cooldown period ensures that every scaling action gets enough time to impact the system's performance positively before any further action. This helps maintain a consistent user experience.

3.3. How to Set Cooldown Periods?

While the default Cooldown period set by cloud providers can be used, it is often recommended to set a specific Cooldown period based on the unique requirements of your application. Here are a few steps on how to set Cooldown periods:

1. Determine the length of time your instances need to be completely operational after they are launched. This could include the time it takes to boot up, run startup scripts, and warm up any caches.

2. After determining the required Cooldown period, you can set it in your auto scaling configuration. This is often done using a command-line interface (CLI) or through the provider's management console.

3. Periodically revisit and adjust the Cooldown period based on any changes to your application's performance, traffic, or scaling

needs.

Remember that the Cooldown period is not a one-size-fits-all solution. It often requires careful monitoring and tweaking to find the optimal balance for your specific use case.

3.4. Challenges with Setting the Cooldown Period

Setting the correct Cooldown period can sometimes present challenges. Here are some common ones:

- `Determining the Right Timing`: Defining the perfect Cooldown period may require trial and error. If the period is set too short, the system might undergo unnecessary scaling in quick successions. If it's too long, the system may not respond quickly enough to changes in demand.

- `Changing Workload Characteristics`: The Cooldown period might have to be adjusted periodically as workload characteristics change. For instance, if your application becomes more efficient and can handle requests quicker, a shorter Cooldown period might suffice.

- `Unexpected Spikes in Demand`: In the event of a sudden increase in traffic, a lengthy Cooldown period could result in under-provisioning and degraded performance. This risk can be mitigated with predictive scaling, effectively foreseeing traffic increases and adjusting resources ahead of time.

3.5. Cooldown vs. Back-to-Back Scaling Activities

A Cooldown period comes handy in preventing back-to-back scaling activities when the load on the system fluctuates between the high and low thresholds in quick successions. Without a Cooldown period, such fluctuations would trigger continuous launching and terminating of instances, resulting in instability and potential performance issues.

Therefore, the Cooldown period serves as a guardrails mechanism, protecting the system from hasty auto scaling reactions that could create chaos and cost inefficiencies.

Although the Cooldown period is a simple concept, its implications on auto scaling and consequently on system performance, cost optimization, and user experience are profound. It's essential to monitor and adjust it based on ongoing system operations and workload characteristics, with an understanding that what works best today might need to be further fine-tuned for the needs of tomorrow.

In the grand scheme of cloud computing and infrastructure management, the Cooldown period may seem as just a small cog. However, it is a cog that keeps the entire auto scaling mechanism working efficiently and smoothly. This is why understanding the Cooldown period and why it matters can make a significant difference in the effective implementation of auto scaling.

Chapter 4. Configuring Cooldown for Optimal Functionality

Auto Scaling Cooldown is an essential component of efficient cloud functioning, ensuring that your services are both responsive and cost-effective. Through a hearty comprehension and configuration of Auto Scaling Cooldown, you can ultimately achieve superior system stability, reduced costs, and a smoother user experience.

4.1. Understanding Auto Scaling Cooldown

One of the first steps on your journey to expertly managing Auto Scaling Cooldown is understanding what it is. In essence, Auto Scaling Cooldown is a period that helps control when your instances can scale out or scale in. This is of vital importance to stop over-provisioning instances, bringing down associated costs and improving efficiency.

It is during this cooldown period that an Auto Scaling group refrains from launching additional instances. It should be noted that cooldowns apply only to simple scaling policies, and they act like a pause between scaling activities to allow your newly launched instances to start handling application traffic.

In terms of time, a default cooldown period is usually set to 300 seconds. This number was chosen because it typically provides enough time to determine whether these new instances are going to help reduce the load on the existing instances. However, this may vary based on the performance of your application and the type of instance you are working with. Remember, this is the time for the system to stabilize, so rushing this process may lead to unstable infrastructures.

4.2. Setting the Cooldown Period

Setting your cooldown period comes down to a balancing act. The configuration process happens through either the management console, command-line interface (CLI), or an AWS SDK. Here's a simple step-by-step guide:

1. Open your Auto Scaling group.

2. In the 'Details' tab, choose 'Edit'.

3. For 'Cooldown', replace the existing amount with your desired period in seconds.

4. Click 'Update' to save your settings.

While setting a cooldown period, question whether a longer or shorter cooldown period benefits your environment. A shorter cooldown period could lead to faster scale-in and scale-out activities, but at the risk of an unstable infrastructure if done too quickly. On the other hand, a longer cooldown period may provide more stability but could also result in an over-provisioning of resources.

4.3. Instance Warm-up

The concept of instance warm-up is closely related to Auto Scaling Cooldown. It represents the amount of time it takes for an instance to bootstrap and be able to serve traffic. Its importance becomes immensely clear when you start seeing applicable charges from the moment an instance is launched, regardless of whether it's ready to handle the load or not.

To avoid unnecessary costs, ensure your instances have appropriate warm-up times, and that these are factored into your cooldown periods. This ensures that instances are only scaled in or scaled out when they are completely set up and ready to handle traffic.

4.4. Understanding Default and Custom Cooldowns

Most of us start with the default cooldown period provided by AWS, which is compressed into an auto scaling group. But does that suffice or should we opt for custom cooldowns? The answer lies in the nature of your applications and their traffic patterns.

A default cooldown meets the requirements of a majority of applications. However, if your application does not begin to take traffic as soon as it's up or has a complex setup process, you may need to tailor a custom cooldown period that fits your specific needs. To do this, simply define a 'Cooldown' period with your desired number of seconds in your scaling policy.

4.5. Monitoring and Adjusting Cooldowns

Monitoring your cooldown periods and adjusting them is critical in maintaining a robust, cost-effective infrastructure. AWS CloudWatch is a handy tool you can use for this. It allows you to monitor your applications and react to system-wide changes in near real-time.

Keep an eye on metrics like 'CPU Utilization', 'Network I/O', 'Disk I/O', and more. If you see consistent over-provisioning of instances, consider analyzing your cooldown periods. They might be too short, causing rapid scaling activities and therefore higher costs.

Likewise, if you are under-provisioning, a shorter cooldown period might be more beneficial. Just remember that changes need to be tested thoroughly and rolled out incrementally to avoid any sudden system shocks.

Remember, Auto Scaling Cooldown is not a one-time set-up but a recurring task requiring frequent monitoring and adjustments. But once mastered, it has the potential to greatly enhance the efficiency and cost-effectiveness of your cloud applications.

In the end, configuring Auto Scaling Cooldown is a journey, and with the guidelines provided, you are now ready to embark on it. Tweak, test, and reiterate until you find the perfect balance for your unique cloud infrastructure. Through a deep understanding and configuring of Auto Scaling Cooldown, it is possible to ensure smooth sailing in the cloud.

Input, feedback and collaboration are essential in this ever-evolving field. So, let's continue the conversation, share our experiences, and collectively enhance our understanding and operation of Auto Scaling Cooldown, an integral player in the dynamic cloud computing world.

Chapter 5. Auto Scaling Policies and Their Impact on Cooldown

Let's begin by comprehending the primary concepts surrounding Auto Scaling Policies and how they directly influence the cooldown process.

5.1. Understanding Auto Scaling Policies

Auto Scaling Policies are essentially rules that adjust the number of instances in response to specific workloads or demands. There are several types of policies, the most common of which are: Target Tracking, Step Scaling, and Simple Scaling. The critical differences among these policies lie in their response to fluctuations in demand.

Target Tracking Scaling automatically adjusts the number of instances based on a specific metric like CPU utilization. For instance, if the aim is to maintain a CPU utilization of 50%, the policy will either launch or terminate instances to meet that target.

Step Scaling and Simple Scaling policies, on the other hand, increase or decrease the capacity in response to alarm thresholds. For example, in Step Scaling, you can define an alarm for CPU utilization above 70% and another for under 30%. Once these thresholds are violated, it would affect the instances according to the corresponding steps defined.

5.2. The Role of Cooldown in Auto Scaling Policies

The idea of cooldown in the context of Auto Scaling is to prevent your cloud infrastructure from a yo-yo effect of constant scale out (launch) and scale in (termination) events.

If there wasn't an Auto Scaling Cooldown period, your system could potentially launch and terminate instances ad nauseam, leading to inefficient utilization of resources.

During the cooldown period, Auto Scaling ensures that the system is not accepting any new scale in or scale out requests. This period allows the instances to start serving traffic and reach their expected performance levels before another scaling activity occurs.

5.3. Configuring Auto Scaling Cooldown Period

The configuration of the Auto Scaling cooldown period varies depending on the chosen scaling policy.

For Simple Scaling policies, one can define the default cooldown period, which applies to both scale in and scale out activities. The recommended value is often based on the time your newly launched instances take to start serving traffic.

For Step Scaling and Target Tracking policies, separate cooldown periods can be specified for scale out and scale in activities. This is ideal for workloads that require a different amount of time to ramp up versus cool down.

However, in reality, identifying the perfect cooldown period duration depends on several factors, including the application startup time, termination time, and potential fluctuations in demand.

5.4. Impact of Incorrect Cooldown Settings

Configuring the incorrect cooldown duration can lead to inefficiency, overutilization, or underutilization of resources. Overprovisioning due to a short cooldown period can lead to unnecessary costs, while underprovisioning due to a long cooldown period can result in subpar application performance.

Tailoring the cooldown to the application's needs is vital to optimize costs and performance. It's a delicate balance that requires a keen understanding of your application's behaviour and the specific demands of your workloads.

5.5. Overcoming the Challenges

It can be tricky to pinpoint the optimal settings due to the dynamic nature of capacity requirements. To overcome this challenge, you can take advantage of predictive scaling, which uses machine learning to forecast future demands and adjusts capacity in advance.

In conclusion, Auto Scaling Policies and their associated cooldown periods play a crucial role in ensuring an efficient and cost-effective cloud infrastructure. Understanding and configuring them correctly help pave the way for a robust, scalable infrastructure that caters to ever-changing demand patterns.

No matter the type of application or solution you're running on the cloud, mastering the interplay of auto scaling policies and their cooldown periods is key to maintaining its optimal performance. While the road might seem intricate and sometimes obscure, the rewards in terms of costs savings, improved resource utilization, and enhanced scalability are worth every step.

Chapter 6. Demystifying the Relationship Between Cooldown and Scaling Activities

Understanding the relationship between cooldown and scaling activities involves peeling back the layers of auto scaling, a dynamic and vital feature of cloud infrastructure, which can be complex for some. Let's break it down bit by bit and truly demystify what goes on behind the scenes.

6.1. The Concept of Cooldown

First and foremost, we need to grasp the idea of a cooldown period in the context of auto scaling. The cooldown period is a length of time that an auto scaling group pauses to enable a newly launched or terminated instance to start functioning. During this time, the auto scaling group doesn't execute any other scaling activities.

It's like pouring water into a full glass incrementally, waiting for the water to settle before pouring again, to prevent spilling over. The time spent waiting for the water to settle is the cooldown period.

The cooldown period is necessary when you implement a scaling policy that automatically increases or decreases the number of instances your system uses. The instances in the cloud need time to initialize and start carrying their weight before deciding if you need more power or not.

6.2. Auto Scaling Process

So, let's talk about what triggers these scaling policies. The auto scaling process usually commences because of a CloudWatch alarm—an alert you set to monitor specific metrics over a time frame.

The CloudWatch alarm keeps track of measures such as average CPU utilization, disk reads/writes, or network traffic. When the alarm threshold breaches, it triggers a scaling activity, and instances are either launched or terminated.

After the scaling activity concludes, depending on the scaling policy, the auto scaling group initiates a cooldown period before deciding to implement any more scaling activities.

6.3. Nature of Cooldown Periods

Cooldown periods can take two forms: default cooldown periods and custom cooldown periods. The former is a property of the auto scaling group that applies to all scaling activities in that group, while the latter applies to specific simple scaling policies.

default cooldown period

The default cooldown period applies after any scaling activity and typically lasts for 300 seconds (5 minutes). It gives newly launched instances ample time to start handling application traffic after launch.

custom cooldown period

Custom cooldown periods apply after a specific scaling policy executes. This feature is a boon when different types of scaling activities take varying lengths of time to complete.

6.4. Interplay Between Cooldown and Scaling Activities

Let's bring these concepts together to understand the interplay. As scaling activities occur, whether they're adding or removing instances, the auto scaling group waits for the cooldown period before deciding if more scaling is necessary.

This system creates a safety buffer, preventing premature instance launches or terminations. It considers any additional instances launched and therefore reduces the chance of unnecessary scaling.

For example, if CPU utilization is the CloudWatch metric, a scaling policy could trigger the launch of an instance. After the launch, the system waits for the cooldown period to conclude. During this time, the newly launched instance begins to share the workload, potentially curbing the CPU utilization. This way, the system preempts the need for another instance.

However, if CPU utilization remains high after the cooldown, it indicates the system still requires more resources, which triggers another scaling activity. Conversely, if CPU utilization drops, the system might trigger a scaling down event after the cooldown period, terminating unnecessary instances.

6.5. Challenges

Understanding the relationship between auto scaling cooldown and scaling activities is one thing. Implementing it is another kettle of fish altogether. Here are some potential challenges:

- *Getting the right timing*: Admins might struggle to set the perfect cooldown period. Too short, and you risk executing scaling activities prematurely; too long, and you risk having an insufficient number of instances for an extended period of time or paying for idle instances.

- *Finding the best metric*: Choosing an effective CloudWatch alarm metric can be challenging. CPU usage, network I/O, disk I/O, and custom metrics all have their place.

- *Monitoring the scaling process*: Keeping an eye on your auto scaling activities might prove daunting, particularly as your cloud infrastructure grows.

6.6. Conclusion

The relationship between auto scaling cooldown and scaling activities fervently illustrates how delicate a balance it is, maintaining an efficient and cost-effective cloud infrastructure. Cooldown periods play an integral role in ensuring that scaling activities are both timely and necessary. While mastering them involves understanding your system, choosing the right metrics, and fine-tuning your timing, the benefits of getting it right—optimized resource use, minimized costs, and enhanced system performance—are well worth the effort.

Chapter 7. Impact of Auto Scaling Cooldown on Cost and Performance

In today's highly dynamic and fast-paced cloud environments, the ability to scale resources automatically (auto scaling) is a critical functionality that helps manage costs, adjusting to load changes, and maintaining application availability. A key feature in this process is the use of the Auto Scaling Cooldown parameter — a temporal aspect of auto scaling that controls the rate of scaling activities within an environment. Let's delve deeper into this ubiquitous aspect of cloud computing and explore how it impacts both cost and performance.

7.1. Understanding Cooldown Periods

Auto Scaling Cooldown is somewhat akin to a 'pause button' that prevents any scaling activity immediately following a scaling event. It ensures that previously executed scale actions have completed and the system has stabilized before initiating another scale activity.

Coordinating multiple scaling actions without a cooldown period could lead to 'thrashing', a frequent and uncontrolled scaling that negatively impacts system performance and stability. The cooldown period also prevents costs from spiraling up due to continuous and unnecessary scale activities. In this context, the Auto Scaling Cooldown is a guardrail that keeps the scale activities in check, ensuring balance and avoiding wastage of resources.

7.2. Impact of Auto Scaling Cooldown on Cost

The Auto Scaling Cooldown significantly contributes to cost management in a cloud environment. Being a critical determinant of when and how subsequent scaling actions occur, it directly influences the resources' consumption and, subsequently, the costs associated with it.

1. Resource Efficiency: A well-configured cooldown can lead to efficient use of resources, thereby helping to reduce your cloud spending. An excessively short cooldown might trigger premature scaling activities, leading to unnecessary resource allocation and wastage. Conversely, a long cooldown could resist necessary scaling, leading to resource underutilization and degraded performance, which ultimately impact business outcomes negatively.

2. Predictability: A well-calibrated cooldown can be instrumental in creating predictability in the cost structure of your cloud environment. A predictable cooldown aids in efficient planning for resource allocation and budgeting. It provides a better picture of resource usage patterns that helps formulate cost-effective scaling strategies.

7.3. Impact of Auto Scaling Cooldown on Performance

The Auto Scaling Cooldown is equally crucial in maintaining and improving the performance of the cloud environment. Here are a few ways it contributes to performance:

1. Stability: As already mentioned, an adequately timed cooldown can prevent thrashing, ensuring system stability post-scaling

operation. An unstable system with frequent scaling can degrade performance and affect availability.

2. Responsiveness: A carefully configured cooldown helps maintain a cloud system's responsiveness to workload changes. Premature scaling or delay in scaling can reduce system responsiveness, leading to sub-optimal performance.

3. End-User Experience: The direct impact of performance is on the end-user. A poorly configured cooldown could lead to slower response times, page load errors, or system unavailability, ultimately reducing the quality of the user experience.

7.4. Cooldown Strategies for Cost and Performance Optimization

There's no single cooldown strategy that fits all scenarios. However, the following principles can guide the configuration of the optimal cooldown period:

1. Understand Workload Patterns: Regularly review your application workload patterns, including peaks, troughs, and trends. This will help you identify when scaling activities happen most and optimize the cooldown period accordingly.

2. Employ Grace Periods: Consider using grace periods, a specific type of cooldown period following an instance's launching. It allows the instance time to boot and applications to fully install before starting another scale-out activity.

3. Dynamic vs. Fixed Cooldown: Depending on your workloads, a dynamic cooldown (where the value changes based on previous scaling actions) could be more useful than a fixed one.

4. Continual Evaluation: Like all cloud-based parameters, the cooldown period should be continually evaluated and adjusted as needed. Regular tuning of this parameter will help keep costs managed and performance optimized.

The impact of the Auto Scaling Cooldown on cost and performance is formidable, and thus, understanding it is crucial for anyone dealing with the world of cloud computing. If configured correctly, it can act as a powerful lever for cost optimization and performance enhancement. With the right strategies and understanding, you can harness its potential and make your cloud environment more balanced, cost-effective, and high-performing.

Chapter 8. Common Challenges in Cooldown Configuration

The auto scaling cooldown feature is a critical component to consider when setting up an auto scaling group in a cloud environment. It essentially provides a buffer—a hiatus, if you will—that controls the rate at which the auto-scaling software provisions or de-provisions resources based on load or performance metrics. But configuring it correctly poses its own challenges. In this report, we will explore some of the most common complications and how to address them for optimum system performance.

8.1. Incorrect Cooldown Period

Arguably, the most common misstep when configuring auto-scaling cooldown is inappropriately setting the cooldown period. If the period is too short, the system becomes prone to rapid, potentially disruptive scaling; if it's too long, the application may suffer from inadequate resources during peak traffic.

The key lies in understanding the nature of your workload. Time-sensitive applications might require quicker scaling to meet the demands of their high load periods, necessitating a shorter cooldown period. On the other hand, applications with relatively stable traffic could benefit from a longer cooldown period.

Measure how long it takes your instance to become fully functional and increase that length to determine your minimum cooldown time. To tune this configuration, run load tests and evaluate the system's response in high-traffic scenarios.

8.2. Misconceptions about the Cooldown Period

It's often misunderstood that the cooldown period is to allow the newly launched instances time to start-up. Rather, its purpose is to suspend additional scaling actions long enough to allow previous load balancing activities to take effect.

Moreover, cooldown is not a pause between individual scaling processes. Instead, it is the time it takes for the system to take observable benefit from the last scaling activity. Keep in mind, if another trigger causes a new scaling during the cooldown period, the scale will take place if the cooldown period of the previous scale has ended. Understanding these nuances will help you configure your cooldown settings correctly.

8.3. Lack of Divergent Configuration for Scaling In and Out

By default, both scaling-in and scaling-out use the same cooldown period. However, 'In' and 'Out' scaling processes can require different amounts of time before they start benefiting the system.

Scaling out (instance launch) usually has a longer cooldown since new instances take a while to start and also need time to accommodate incoming traffic. On the flip side, scaling in (instance termination) mostly requires a shorter cooldown as the impact of instance termination is quicker, and the load balancer can rapidly redistribute the traffic.

Once you understand these distinctions, adjust your configurations to use separate, customizable cooldown periods for scaling in and scaling out.

8.4. The Overlooked Adjustment Types

When configuring your auto scaling group, it is crucial to understand and correctly choose the adjustment type—percentage change in capacity or number of instances added or removed. Often people stick to the default settings, which may not always be effective.

A percentage-based adjustment type provides flexibility as it scales according to the change in load. Using the number of instances as the adjustment type may not be as efficient if your application encounters sudden surges or plunges of traffic. However, using a fixed number of instances can offer predictability.

When it comes to cooldown periods, consider that percentage-based adjustments may need a longer cooldown to absorb the traffic, while fixed quantity adjustments might work with shorter cooldown periods.

8.5. Neglecting Cloud Provider's Cooldown Defaults

It's common to overlook the default cooldown configurations provided by your cloud provider. While these defaults are generally universally applicable, they may not always suffice, particularly if your application is subject to significant traffic.

In such cases, you might benefit from configuring additional, application-specific cooldown periods, which largely provide more control over your scaling activities. Evaluating your application's performance under different load scenarios will guide you to a more tailor-made cooldown strategy.

In conclusion, engineering an optimal cooldown regimen isn't so much a science as it is an art, requiring a keen understanding of the system in question and an intuitive approach. Comprehending these common challenges and how to counteract them will vastly simplify your configuration ordeal, making your cloud environment even more efficient and resilient.

Remember that the field of cloud scaling is fluid and ask you to maintain an ongoing commitment to learning and adaptation. Keep reassessing your configuration in response to changing circumstances—testing, experimenting, and attuning. It's a journey rather than a destination. Happy configuring!

Chapter 9. Solving Troubles: A Deep Dive into Cooldown-related Problems

As we delve deeper into the realm of Auto Scaling Cooldown, it's necessary to understand that this intricate mechanism may, at times, come with its own set of challenges. Encountering problems is part of the learning curve, and if you're not witnessing any, you're most likely not exploring enough. So, let's assume you're a brave explorer in the field, and we're going to help you navigate through this maze of cooldown-related problems with a virtually unerring compass.

9.1. Overcooling: The Ice Age of Auto Scaling

Overcooling, though it might sound like a pleasant excess in some contexts, in the landscape of auto scaling, it's one of the problems that can lead to unnecessary runtime dormancy, thereby affecting your cloud computing efficiencies.

Imagine a scenario where you have a cooldown period that's too long: your instances are idle for more time than required post-scaling operations, leading to loss in efficiency. This excess "cool off" period doesn't just reduce performance, but might also result in financial wastage, as you're still paying for the idle resources.

To avoid overcooling, it's important to perform a detailed analysis of your application's normal operations and calculate a sensible cooldown value. Monitor your applications to understand the time it typically takes for them to stabilize after a scaling activity, and set your cooldown periods accordingly.

9.2. Undercooling: When It's Too Hot for Comfort

The flip side of overcooling is undercooling. As the name suggests, this occurs when the cooldown period is too short. In such a scenario, your systems might not get ample time to stabilize post an auto scaling event before the next trigger kicks in. This can potentially lead to frequent scaling of instances, thereby stressing the system unnecessarily.

To address undercooling, follow a similar prescription as for overcooling: careful monitoring of your system's behavior after a scaling activity. This helps in determining the ideal cooldown period that allows enough respite without slowing things down unduly.

9.3. The Balance Beam: Striking the Right Cooldown Period

Balancing the cooldown period is a key aspect of configuring auto scaling. Neither too hot nor too cold - it's the Goldilocks principle playing out in cloud infrastructure.

Achieving this equilibrium requires analytical finesse. You need to delicately balance between cost efficiency and your application's performance. One helpful strategy lies in running simulations to model your application's behavior under a variety of scenarios. You can then assess the impact of scaling operations, allowing you to derive an ideal cooldown period.

9.4. The Challenge of Dynamic Workloads

The cloud is a dynamic playground, with workloads witnessing deep valleys of relative inactivity, followed by peaks of acute demand almost instantaneously. These fluctuations can pose unique challenges for setting cooldown periods.

Dynamic workloads require adaptive cooldown periods. Automatic adjustments based on real-time factors is one way to go. Third-party auto scaling tools often offer a feature known as 'dynamic cooldowns', which adjust the cooldown period based on the current processing load and traffic patterns.

9.5. Unpredictable Traffic Surges: The "Black Friday Syndrome"

Black Friday, Cyber Monday, seasonal sales, special events – your cloud infrastructure might be hit by sudden traffic surges during such events. While auto scaling is designed to handle increased load, if not configured correctly, this may lead to an auto scaling cooldown problem commonly known as the "Black Friday Syndrome", where systems struggle to keep scale up and down in response to the rapid fluctuations.

Understanding your business cycle and associate traffic trends can go a long way here. Forecasting such traffic surges and planning for them in advance can help you steer your auto scaling configuration in the right direction and avoid cooldown mishaps during these critical periods.

In conclusion, troubleshooting cooldown-related problems is a core skill in managing auto scaling. As you set sail on this voyage of configuring and managing Auto Scaling Cooldown, remember to monitor, analyze, iterate, learn, and adapt. Patience and analytical acumen will be your best allies, and with them, you're well-equipped to tackle the challenges head on and keep your cloud infrastructure in optimum working condition.

Chapter 10. Real-world Case Studies of Cooldown Misconfigurations & Solutions

Even during our best-laid plans, things can occasionally go amiss, and understanding how certain missteps lead to failures can provoke expansive learning. With that in mind, we'll delve into a few intriguing real-world scenarios where cooldown misconfigurations have played a significant role. In each case, we'll outline the particular misconfiguration that occurred, the impact of the error, and potential solutions and best practices to prevent such issues in the future.

10.1. Misconfiguration Case Study 1: Over-aggressive Scaling

In this scenario, a tech company running a large-scale data processing application experienced recurrent performance issues. The problem was traced back to an overly aggressive auto-scaling cooldown configuration. The autoscaling cooldown time was set to a bare minimum of one minute. Consequently, the system reduced or increased instances almost immediately after a spike or dip in demand.

This configuration led to two interconnected issues. One problem was that the rapid response to traffic changes induced instability because the newly provisioned instances were not given enough time to warm up and handle requests efficiently. Secondly, and significantly, the company faced a surge in resource consumption costs due to the continuous provisioning and decommissioning of instances.

The resolution involved increasing the cooldown time to allow instances enough warming-up time and to steady the erratic load-balancing. They also implemented predictive scaling based on previously observed traffic, which helped buffer sudden fluctuations in load.

10.2. Misconfiguration Case Study 2: Inadequate Cooldown Time

Another case involved a renowned e-commerce platform. The company had their auto-scaling configured with a low cooldown time. This resulted in auto-scaling actions getting triggered too frequently, leading to a constant cycle of scaling-in and scaling-out.

The costs incurred due to unnecessary instance termination and initiation were of concern. More critically, however, was the user experience, which took a significant hit as availability fluctuated, causing intermittent disturbance to shoppers on the site.

Adjusting the cooldown time to a sensible value, combined with removing cyclic dependencies in the auto-scaling process, solved the issue. The improved system used a scaling policy considering response time and CPU usage, helping keep the service available and reliable.

10.3. Misconfiguration Case Study 3: Ignoring Cold Starts

A leading News app with global popularity fell into the trap of ignoring the cold-start issue. In anticipation of high traffic during breaking news, they had set up an auto-scaling policy with a short cooldown time. While this setup catered to the demand surges, it didn't take into account the 'cold starts' each new instance experienced. The time an instance takes to become fully operational—'cold start'—had not been factored into the cooldown time.

This oversight led to periods of underperformance when the user demand was high, tarnishing the user experience precisely when most users were on the app.

By lengthening the cooldown time to account for 'cold starts' and employing predictive scaling mechanisms, the app was able to handle traffic surges without compromising on performance or user experience.

Understanding auto-scaling in the context of real-world applications with real-world problems can provide fresh insights into how cooldown settings can significantly affect the smooth functioning and cost-effectiveness of your cloud infrastructure. In the case studies above, the recurring theme is understanding your application's load patterns and taking the time to fine-tune your cooldown settings. With best practices in place and regular monitoring, successful, efficient auto-scaling is attainable.

Chapter 11. Future Perspectives on Auto Scaling and Cooldown Management

Auto scaling and cooldown mechanisms have been disrupting the field of cloud computing since their inception. They have not just transformed the way cloud-based systems and applications operate, but have also laid the path for future innovations. This chapter is dedicated to outlining some of the future perspectives on auto scaling and cooldown management. Drawn from expert predictions, current trends, and in-depth research, the discussion ventures into potential advancements and challenges in this area.

11.1. The Rise of Context-Aware Auto Scaling

As technology evolves, so does the sophistication of computing resources. One potential advancement is the integration of context-aware systems in auto scaling. These systems, already making a significant impact in other digital areas, may be used to improve decision-making processes around auto scaling and cooldowns.

Context-aware auto scaling refers to the ability of a system to adjust resource allocation based on specific conditions or contexts. This mechanism can predict demand, taking into account different situational factors such as traffic fluctuations, system load, or specific user behavior. By leveraging machine learning algorithms and predictive analytics, context-aware auto scaling could provide a more accurate, real-time response, thereby enhancing system efficiency and performance.

11.2. Hybrid Cloud and Auto Scaling

Hybrid cloud has been gaining traction as a future-proof model for IT infrastructures. With the key advantage of seamlessly blending private and public cloud functionalities, the hybrid cloud presents interesting opportunities for auto scaling.

In a hybrid cloud setting, managing auto scaling can be more complex due to the distribution of resources across different environments. However, it also presents the possibility of enhanced scheduling and allocation of workloads across multiple cloud platforms. A carefully configured auto scaling policy, coupled with an efficient cooldown mechanism, can ensure optimal resource utilization while taking advantage of the scalability, flexibility, and cost-effectiveness of multiple cloud environments.

11.3. AI and ML in Cooldown Management

Artificial Intelligence (AI) and Machine Learning (ML) have permeated almost every digital domain, and it's not a far stretch to envision their integration into auto scaling and cooldown management. AI and ML can be exploited to learn from historical data, discern patterns, and make intelligent decisions about when to scale up or down, thereby improving both system performance and cost efficiency.

By using ML algorithms, it might be possible to predict sharp demand surges or drops before they occur, enabling preemptive scaling actions. AI could also be leveraged for effective cooldown management, ensuring that the systems do not scale down too quickly after a scale-up operation, which could cause performance issues.

11.4. Security Considerations

With the increasing reliance on auto scaling and cooldown mechanisms, comes a greater need for robust security measures. Provisioning and de-provisioning instances on a large scale opens up potential points of vulnerability that attackers might exploit.

Future developments in auto scaling and cooldown management must therefore prioritize the creation of secure auto scaling groups, enhancing security protocols, and employing advanced algorithms to detect and counteract potential security threats efficiently. It won't be surprising if we see a convergence of auto scaling technologies with cutting-edge cybersecurity measures, resulting in more secure, resilient systems.

11.5. The Evolution of User Interfaces

As auto scaling becomes more ingrained in cloud operations, we can expect to see enhancements in user interfaces designed to manage auto scaling and cooldowns. A more interactive and user-friendly UI would enable even less tech-savvy individuals to efficiently monitor and control auto scaling processes. These improvements might include elaborate dashboards with real-time performance metrics or more intuitive features for adjusting auto scaling policies.

While predictions about the future can't be made with complete certainty, the trends suggest that auto scaling and cooldown management will continue to evolve, driving efficiencies in cloud computing. The focus will be not only on managing resources and cost but also on improving security, enabling predictive scaling, and enhancing user experience. The journey to these future advancements remains a fascinating process, full of opportunities and challenges that will shape the next chapters of auto scaling and cooldown management.